beloved,

mathias maurin
www.mathiasmaurin.com

dedicated to you,
the beloved

beloved,

"We love because He first loved us."

1 John 4:19 (ESV)

a letter to the reader

-///-

beloved,

What comes to mind when you read this word? It is a beautiful word and it means *dearly loved,* or *a much loved person.*

John, in His gospel, refers to himself as *the disciple whom Jesus loved.* When I first read this, it seemed arrogant, even a little narcissistic: How could John single himself out like that? How could he claim such a thing?

This title grabbed me and wouldn't let go. How could John be so confident, so steely, so sure of himself? After sitting for a while with the words, though, I've come to see that John wasn't simply singling himself out, but stating a universe-shaping reality: "I am the one whom Jesus loves."

To believe anything less is to silence the work of the cross. Surely, if the cross could speak to us, it would say "You are the one whom Jesus loves." John literally *saw* Jesus suffer and die on the cross. He saw it and understood what it meant: I am loved by God, creator of the universe. Having seen this with his own eyes, he wrote what so many have now heard and memorized: "For *God so loved* the world, that He gave His one and only Son..." (John 3:16 NIV) I so easily believe the cross to be the center of history and the most powerful cosmic event that has ever happened. Do I also believe with the same conviction that *I am the one whom Jesus loves?*

This is the Gospel: your belovedness. Why did Jesus endure the cross? For no other reason than His love for you. Imagine beholding the cross and then turning around and saying "Who am I to believe that I am the one whom Jesus loves?" This is the truly arrogant response.

When we claim our utter belovedness, we claim that we are powerless to *gain* our salvation: Jesus didn't go to the cross because we deserved it, or earned it, or worked for it, but because we are the ones He loves.

This is the story of the Bible: our belovedness. Read it and find that we are the *bride* of Christ, the *children* of God, the *friends* of Jesus.

Beloved one, the journey with Jesus is simply a journey deeper and deeper into the realization that you are truly *the one whom Jesus loves*. We can only realize this reality as we enter into relationship with Him, spending time with Him and His Word, inviting Him to change us, and making ourselves available to Him and His work. As we live in the implications of this reality we come to understand that obedience makes sense, that God, because He loves us, is worthy of our trust, and that those around us are beloved, too. While at first belovedness may seem like an arrogant cop-out, it actually becomes the center and key to a genuine, loving, and humble Christ-centered life. Jesus Himself lived from the place of being utterly loved by Father and Spirit, and this was the source of His direction, miracles, and strength.

-///-

I wrote the following meditations in response to a pain I found within me, a pain that led me into a deep darkness and a genuine grief, a pain that fought against the voice that called me the beloved, tempting me to disbelieve. These reflections, like glimmers of starlight or the first rays of dawn, gave me a hope I could lean into. They are the distillations of ideas learned from experience, conversations with spiritual mentors, interactions with the Word, and times of contemplative prayer.

They are short and simple because I needed them to be. They were written as reminders to myself as I waded through the darkness around me, heard the conflicting voices of pain and love, and waited on the newness that comes with healing.

I quickly began to realize that the only way through all of this was to journey deeper into belovedness. Still, I often struggle to reconcile the disappointment and pain I feel with the reality that I am perfectly loved, and I am sure you, too, experience this struggle.

I invite you to read the following poems slowly, perhaps only reading one or two at a time, and reflect on what they may be asking you to believe or do. Resist the urge, as you read, to gloss over the first (and most important) word of each poem: *beloved*. If this little book contained no other words than *beloved*, it would still be a feast for contemplation.

I pray that these reflections will be helpful in at least some way to you as you journey into the truth of your belovedness. May Jesus meet you in these words.

much love,

the one whom He loves

"Come, anyone who thirsts,
come to the waters;
and he who has no money,
come, buy, and eat!
Come, buy wine and milk
without money and without price.

Why do you spend your money
for that which is not bread,
and your labor for that which does not satisfy?
Listen diligently to me, and eat what is good,
and delight yourselves in rich food."

-The Prophet Isaiah

(Isaiah 55:1-2 ESV)

beloved,
please
allow yourself
to actually
be loved

beloved,
I've been having
a conversation
with your Maker:
He says you're His
favorite.

(He says I am too,
and when you hear Him say it,
it makes perfect sense:
everyone in His family
is His favorite)

would you care to
pull up a chair,
grab a cup
(He'll fill it)
and join us?

beloved,
you are beloved,
whether you think so or not,
whether the other voices agree or not.
when your own judgement says you are not,
can you have the courage
to trust what the Omniscient
calls you?

hear it
in your heartbeat, even now,
"beloved"
"beloved"
"beloved"
each breath you breathe
"beloved"
"beloved"
"beloved"

the life you live
is itself a gift
bought with blood and death.
this very life you live
evidence of this,
your truest nature:
beloved

beloved,
when the wound
within you
insists on being heard
and threatens your peace,
to whom will you first turn?

insist to your own heart
(even when it feels futile)
that your Maker is the
only true source of wholeness

ensure that those
who seek to help you
believe this, too,
and that they do not
attempt to fill
your endless need—
this will only result in
mutual disappointment

oved,
when you feel
that your life is
worthless,
remember how much
He paid for it

beloved,
when you see Him,
run to the place where He is,
paying no mind
to what you leave behind

beloved,
do not allow your fear
of being afraid,
or disappointed,
or just bored,
keep you from entering
the place where He dwells

when the distance
between you feels far,
remember (in grief)
that He is immutable
and
remember (in joy)
that He is omnipresent

beloved,
try to turn
"is He giving me anything?"
into
"what is He giving me?"

perhaps when He isn't
"doing anything"
He is actually
giving
the gift
of silence,
the luxury
of nothing

nothing but Himself,
which is, of course,
everything

beloved,
do not fear silence
for its emptiness,
rather,
ask
what it might be saying
ask
what it might be asking
or simply

be,

remembering that
His silence
is not
His absence

beloved,
some discomfort
should be expected:

sometimes,
light can feel harsh
when you've lived
too long in
darkness

waking up
can be uncomfortable
can even feel unnatural
when you've
been asleep

beloved,
do not be afraid of
your vast neediness;
it is no reason for shame

it may, however,
be a sign
you are bringing your needs
to an insufficient source

one only feels
ravenous
when they seat themselves
at a meager table
(which is often all we
think we deserve)

see the table
set in His house:
a feast of endless love

see Him,
even now,
inviting you in

beloved,
sometimes your desires
distract you from the
One true desire of your heart:
Him

He may not give you
what you think you desire
because he simply
does not want to disappoint you

He (alone) can give what
truly satisfies
and
He (alone) will give
what truly satisfies

beloved,
your Lover
can sometimes feel
far away

it was never meant to be this way,
and it is okay
to feel sad
when you long for
the cool days
and long walks
hand-in-hand
with the One
who feels like (is) home

He shares this sadness,
the sadness of separation,
and is
mending all things

beloved,
it is the work
of the fall
and the fallen one
to convince you that you are not
the beloved.
do not be discouraged
when everything around you
seems to attack you

to believe in the face of grief
is to dethrone
the one who lies

and enthrone
the One who cannot lie,
the One who calls you
beloved

"Behold, I am with you always, to the end of the age."

-Jesus of Nazareth

(Matthew 28:20 ESV)

beloved,
when your heart
feels abandoned,
keep in mind that
alone
is simply an
impossibility
when your Lover
is omnipresent

beloved,
sometimes you do not see Him
because He's asking you
to look

and see
how He's been *here*
the whole time

beloved,
when you struggle
to see the good
do not strain your eyes
or run to a faraway place
in searching.
this will only tire you.

stay here,
believing good is
right in front of you.
you won't find good "over there"
if you can't find it here.
(it may be simpler than you think:
a breath, a beating heart, a ray of sun)

even a sliver of good
is enough to warrant
gratitude,
and gratitude is the gateway
to His house

beloved,
learn to see the
reflection of the Divine
in the gifts
He gives you:
His providence in the meal before you
His joy in that laughing flower
His heart in another

but if, when,
He asks you to let go of
these reflections of His heart,
remember
He will never ask you to let go of
His heart

sometimes,
in giving up
the gift
we are made more able
to know and see
the Giver

beloved,
this journey
of joy and pain,
of gifts given and taken
is all about
learning that
your needs
find their only real fulfilment
in Him.

can you begin to believe
that your longings
are not evidence
of something withheld
but actually holy whispers
beckoning you to
return to
the only One
who satisfies?

"Behold I am making all things new."

-The Enthroned One

(Revelation 21:5 ESV)

beloved,
even *He*
wept

beloved,
sobbing
isn't a betrayal
of hope;
there's nothing
wrong with grieving
the pain you feel,
which is the world's pain,
which is His pain

He, Perfecter of all things,
grieves too

beloved,
do not fear your grief,
or think it always
inappropriate:
to grieve
is a sign
that you have
loved

beloved,
sometimes
the beauty of
what could have been
distracts you from
the beauty of what is:
being with Him

beloved,
that gnawing emptiness
does not need to be
a source of shame,
or a disquiet you must hide from,
but can actually be a reminder of
your utter need for Him,
a vessel only endless Love
can fill

beloved,
learn to cling,
white-knuckled,
to the Giver

but to hold lightly
with open hands,
the gifts He gives

only One
is truly unchanging
only One
is permanent
or, in a different word,
only One is
eternally Given

beloved,
what looks
like amputation
may actually be
pruning

beloved,
may you begin to see
your difficult circumstances
not as punishment
but as opportunities to trust Him
for no other reason
than
utter love of Him

beloved,
do not despise
the hidden work:
the growth of roots
whose progress
remains unseen

a storm may topple a tree,
but it cannot
touch the roots,
those underground branches
from which
new growth
receives its sustenance

a felling
need not be an end,
and the stump which remains
can be a holy seed

beloved,
do not fear
your capacity to feel pain.
for what is pain if not
a portal into
empathy,
compassion,
even,
communion?

do not be offended
if He asks the wound in your heart
to be the birthplace
of a new growth,
a deeper love

beloved,
what will you do
with your pain?
will you hold it,
close to your chest,
and feel it evermore?
a reminder of
"what could have been?"
or will you give it to Him
and let Him breathe new meaning into it
transfiguring it
into something
beautiful?

beloved,
all you

ever truly had

ever truly have

will ever truly have

is Him

beloved,
you will find it
very difficult
(impossible)
to hold onto
both peace
and unforgiveness

which will you
surrender?

beloved,
you may desire
resurrection
(which is beautiful)
but that means
in one way or another
you must first
die

beloved,
remember that
losing your life
is only the first half:

the work is not
complete
until your life
is found anew

do not show off your
self-death
to the world;
the world
will only ravage you

rather,
trust Him with the
nakedness of your death
and He will clothe you
in new life

beloved,
do not fear
your own emptiness—
the poverty of spirit
that gnaws at your
desire to be independent

the recognition of your weakness
is nothing but an opportunity
to put His strength
on full display

beloved,
when you seek control,
remember that control
is (mostly)
an illusion—
can you even tell your own
heart to stop beating?
fingernails to stop growing?
let alone
tell the rain to fall elsewhere?
the clouds to move away?

when you desire to seek control,
seek rather
the One
whose voice the wind obeys,
the One
for Whom that heart of yours
so wildly beats

beloved,
when the storm keeps battering
despite your desperate prayers
for it to stop,
or move on,

perhaps
He is giving you
something better:
a place of permanent Refuge,
asking you to step in,
drawing you
not simply away from evil
but ever closer
to good,
to Himself

beloved,
when grief comes
and threatens to ravage you
the task of your heart is
dwelling in the peace
of His embrace
rather than
ceaselessly searching
to understand

beloved,
being
"resilient"
is hard,

and often those around you
do not understand that
"resilient"
isn't just something you are,
but is actually made of
many difficult choices

do not feel
a need to
be "resilient"
with Him

He can handle
your
unraveling

beloved,
there's no point
in being anything but honest
with Him
He *is* omniscient
after all

come to Him

and uncork:
weep
scream
wrestle
praise
yell
marvel
ask
thank
be

beloved,
the tension you feel
is expected,

for you have tasted
of the reality that
has come in part
and will soon come in fullness

He has planted in you
a tree not meant for the soil
of this world;
of course you
feel a little

homesick

beloved,
being human isn't easy,
and it's okay
to wonder what
the One in control
is doing,
how He's going to
flip this one around
and make good come
from the bad

He understands
(from experience)
the limitations
of body
the pain
of distance
the ambivalence
of humanness,
His very pores crying out,
in the struggle of it,
sweating blood

beloved,
do you *really* think
He would abandon you
after
dying for you?

beloved,
do not give yourself to despair
when your circumstances
look very different
from your past experience
or your idea
of belovedness

remember,
the most costly gift of love,
the gift that gave you life,
looked like death
for a few days

remember,
and tell your heart that
His promises say more about reality
than your circumstances

beloved,
it may be hard
for you to hear,
but understanding
is not
a prerequisite of
obedience

beloved,
if you feel you
are catching no fish,
do not despair that the
waters are empty

perhaps
He is asking you
to shift your perspective,
to cast your net on the other side

perhaps
He is setting the scene
for an abundance
you could not have imagined,
an abundance realized
through simple obedience
alone

beloved,
when you ask for light
to break your darkness
and for blessings
to fill your hands

ensure your
eyes and hands are
actually open,
ready to receive
what you've asked for
keeping in mind,
it might not look as
you expected
(but trust Him,
it will always be
better in the end)

beloved,
why do you so often
expect
this to look like something
extraordinary

when He said it looks like
the field of wheat
the yeast in bread
the fisherman on the waters

bring Him your
mustard seed
and, no matter how slowly,
ordinarily,
He will make it grow

beloved
the longing
which will not
be satisfied

is a longing for
Him

as you learn to
live with Him
and, on that precious day,
when you *see* Him,

it will be satisfied

beloved,
when you are frustrated
that He is not here,
or, at least,
that His body is not here,
hear Him
call you blessed
because you believe
and love
though you have not seen Him

when He invited the doubter
to touch His wounds,
He thought of you

beloved,
when confusion strikes
and you can't reconcile
your situation
with your idea of belovedness,
come back to the Crux of it
and see that
the One who died for you
knows how to
lead you into good,
and is worthy of your trust

beloved,
what could you need
when He has promised
His whole heart?

when you doubt,
behold the contract
of this Ancient Love,
signed
in nails and blood

beloved,
listen to them,
hear their unified voice,
the roots of the swaying trees,
the infant at the breast,
the petals of sunsoaked flowers,
the primal beating of your heart,
the pull of the universe:
hold on
if only to the corner of His robe,
do not let go
of the Light that
reveals
who you truly are

beloved,
do not be afraid to
ask for a miracle

but do not be surprised
if it isn't immediately obvious,
if it looks "ordinary,"
if it happens slowly,
if He asks you to play a part

His grandest miracle,
His answer to a world of
darkness
was a feeble Baby,
a normal Carpenter,
a gruesome execution,
before it ever
looked like
an answer

beloved,
He knows
what you need
(even better than you do)
and He is in control

beloved,
if faced with a choice,
and He is giving
no answer at all,
perhaps, could it be possible,
that He wants you to choose?

make your choice,
always choosing to move
with Him,
whatever you do.

He will never do
any abandoning.

and do not fear failure.
after all,
redeemed one,
with Him,
failure
is never
final

beloved,
you are free
from anything
that keeps you
from Him

beloved,
if you feel that
you are running out

of love to give,
please consider
whether the source
of what you give
is actually
the Source of Love

if not,
direct your effort
to returning
to the True Source
and watch
your heart
overflow

beloved,
you have no greater calling than

to experience Love,

be changed by Love,

and give Love in return

beloved,
when someone is thirsty
by all means
give them a cup
of your water

remembering that,
though it can feel
validating to provide,
your true task is
pointing,
not providing—

show the thirsty
to the River,
how to drink
from the Source,
the *real* Provider,
to an abundance
they may not have thought
possible—
to never thirst again

beloved,
the evil one's
capacity to steal
will never match
(or even come close to)
your Lover's power to give

behold,
evil's greatest weapon:
death.
behold,
our Lover's greatest work:
killing death

beloved,
is He trustworthy?
is He loving?
your answer
may be
the difference between
peace and despair

no matter how
complicated they may become,
your surroundings
do not have the power
to answer these
questions for you

only you do

beloved,
in seeking what is right,
how to obey,
do not neglect to seek
the face
the heart
the presence
of the only One
who can tell you

sometimes,
He does not answer your
practical questions
because

He would rather
be loved, adored, enjoyed,
by your true self
than served, obeyed, neglected
by your self-righteousness

He will not encourage
an obedience
that does not find its source
in trust,
in love

beloved,
He knocks
at the door of this moment,
every moment,
longing to be with you
(for with Him is where you belong,
the secret cry of your heart)

can you see the journey
He has made to
the house of your heart?
see all that He gave up,
yes, even His life,
for the chance to
knock at your door.

There is no pressure,
but always, there is a choice.
will you invite Him in,
and turn your heart to
the One who makes
you whole?

beloved,
please allow yourself
to actually
be loved

"The Spirit and the bride say 'Come.'
And let the one who hears say, 'Come.'
And let the one who is thirsty come;
let the one who desires
take the water of life without price."

-Revelation 22:17 ESV

mathias maurin
www.mathiasmaurin.com

Made in the USA
Las Vegas, NV
31 August 2022

54441137R00046